ANCIENT
EGYPTIANS
Sticker Book

D1711671

Licensed exclusively to Top That Publishing Ltd
Tide Mill Way, Woodbridge, Suffolk, IP12 IAP, UK
www.topthatpublishing.com
Copyright © 2017 Tide Mill Media
All rights reserved
2 4 6 8 9 7 5 3 1
Manufactured in Zhejiang, China

The fertile Nile

The Nile, the longest river in the world, was the key to the 3,000-year history of Ancient Egypt. Its annual flooding made the surrounding land fertile and the river itself was used for fishing, transport and trade. Ancient Egypt's population and all of its important buildings were situated close to the Nile.

Egyptians used dogs for hunting.

Stick a hungry hippo here!

In Ancient Egypt, the Nile didn't really have a name. It was just called "the river."

Hungry hippos did a lot of damage to crops.

Traders imported wood, spices, incense trees, and leopard skins.

Stick an angry hippo here!

Nile crocodile
Up to 20 feet long, eats fish, birds, mammals, and unlucky fishermen!

Egyptian agriculture

The agricultural year was divided into three seasons: flooding, planting, and harvest. The Nile allowed Egyptians to grow a wide variety of fruits and vegetables, as well as flax to make rope and clothes, and papyrus to make writing material. Animals were kept for their meat, milk and skins, and to work the land.

Above the river, fruit such as dates, grapes, and watermelons were grown. They were fertilized with pigeon poop!

Canals were dug to make the most of the yearly flooding and to extend the irrigated areas.

Barley was used for bread and beer. Hic!

Ducks and geese were kept and fed with dough to fatten them up.

Nets were used for hunting waterfowl.

Ancient gods

Religion in Ancient Egypt was very complicated! There were over 2,000 gods linked to different regions, animals, or professions. Not everyone believed the same stories, and gods changed in importance over time, or even merged with other gods.

Stick Osiris' crown here!

I'm Osiris, god of the afterlife. I was king, but my brother Set plotted against me, and killed me...twice! The second time he cut me into little pieces. Charming!

I'm Horus, god of vengeance, war, and hunting. I battled Set to avenge my father Osiris, and to decide who ruled Egypt. I won!

I'm Isis, goddess of health, marriage, and love. I'm Osiris' sister...and wife! With Anubis' help, I brought Osiris back to life.

I'm Anubis, god of mummification and embalming, and protector of the dead.

Finish Anubis' scepter!

I'm Set, god of storms, disorder, and violence...but I'm not all bad! I help the sun god, Ra, on his nightly battle with the evil snake god, Apep!

Everyday life

Most houses were built of sun-baked mud bricks. Wood wasn't an option, as trees were rare, and stone was expensive. This stone house belongs to a rich official and has a garden and a pond. Houses had open-air kitchens and flat roofs—great for sleeping on in hot weather.

Add a wind-catcher!

Windcatchers helped keep houses cool. Some funneled the air through wet linen—early air conditioning!

Stick a mother and child here!

Ball games, wrestling, throwing games, and board games, like "senet," were all popular.

Only a few lucky boys went to school. Girls stayed at home and poor boys helped on farms.

The punishment for killing a cat was the death penalty! If a cat died, its owners shaved their eyebrows off, to show how upset they were!

The "sidelock of youth" was shaved off at about 12-14 years old. You had to start wearing clothes then too...boo!

Pet hoopoe

Stick a sneaky cat here!

Most sandals were made of papyrus. These more expensive ones were made of leather.

Djoser's giant steps 2648 BC

The Egyptians started to build incredible stone structures over 4,000 years ago. Pharaoh Djoser built the first recognizable pyramid in Saqqara. His "step pyramid" was the largest building of its time and was a similar size to a typical town! Pyramids weren't just monuments...they included everything the pharaoh needed for the afterlife.

The 30-foot high outer walls had 15 doors, but only one opened, the rest were false! A 130-foot wide trench surrounded the walls.

The Heb Sed Court

Add a throne here!

The djed pillar symbolized the spine of Osiris and was raised at the beginning of the Heb Sed festival.

Priest

Burial chambers for the pharaoh and his family were not in the pyramid, but under it... nearly 100 feet deep!

The pyramid complex was also used for ceremonies. In this one, the pharaoh ran between two markers to show he was still fit enough to rule!

Marker stone

The Great Pyramid (around 2570 BC)

Inspired by the step pyramid of Djoser, Khufu built the enormous "Great Pyramid." It took thousands of workers over 20 years to build.
No pharaoh ever built anything as large again, and for almost 4,000 years it remained the tallest man-made structure in the world!

The Great Pyramid
Height: 480 feet
Area: 756 x 756 feet

Khafre's Pyramid
Height: 471 feet
Area: 706 x 706 feet

Menkaure's Pyramid
Height: 215 feet
Area: 335 x 343 feet

55 ton granite blocks, for the "King's Chamber," were transported from more than 500 miles away!

Building a pyramid wasn't easy and required tens of thousands of men—both skilled and unskilled workers.

Doctors were kept busy with broken bones and other injuries.

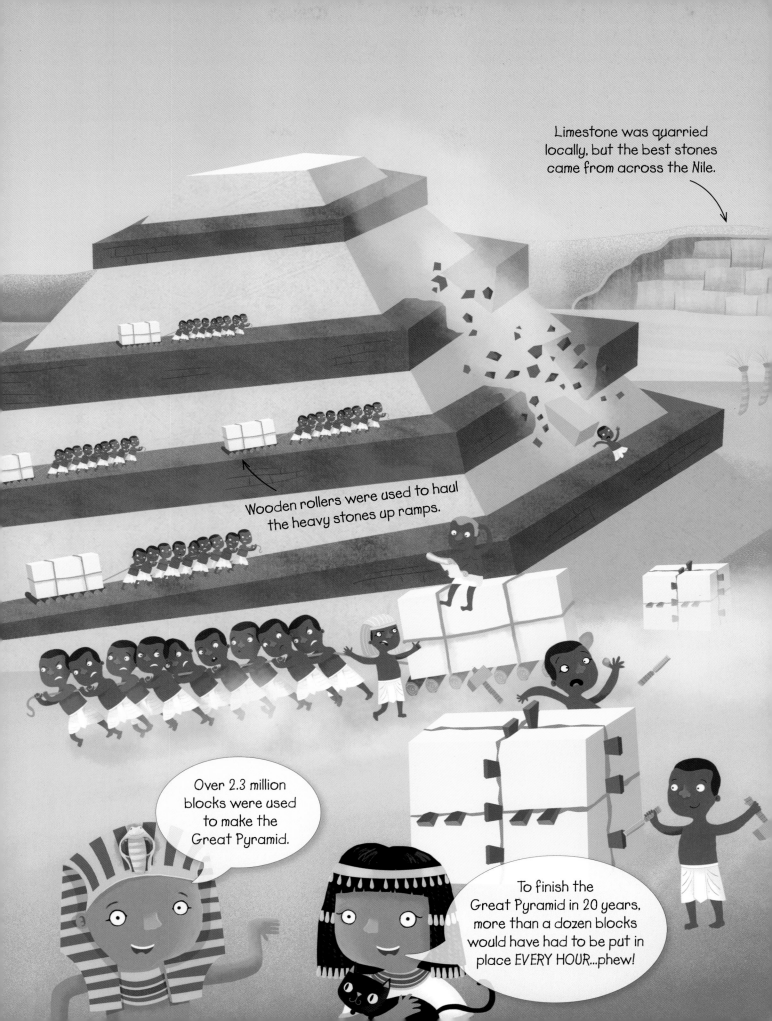

Create your own Great Pyramid sticker scene!

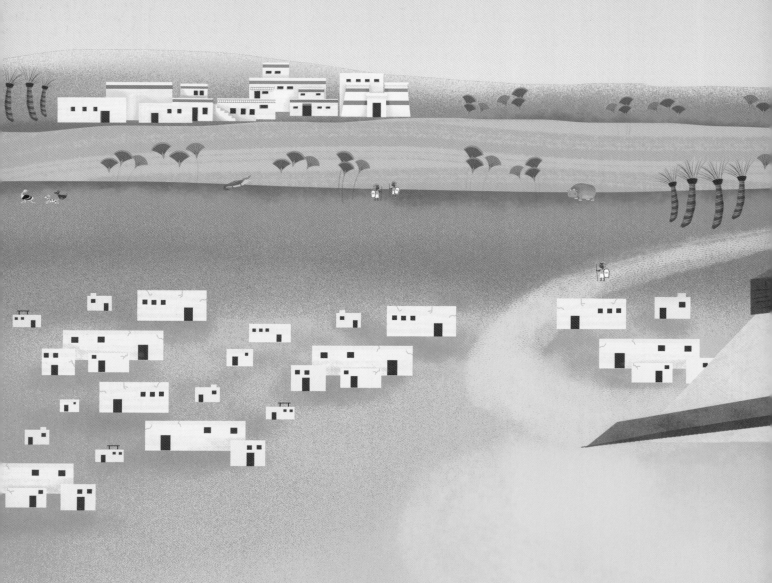

Inside the pyramid

The inside of the Great Pyramid is just as fascinating as the outside, but, once it was closed, no one was ever supposed to see it. After the pharaoh's funeral, the entrance shaft was sealed with huge granite stones, and the entrance was carefully concealed.

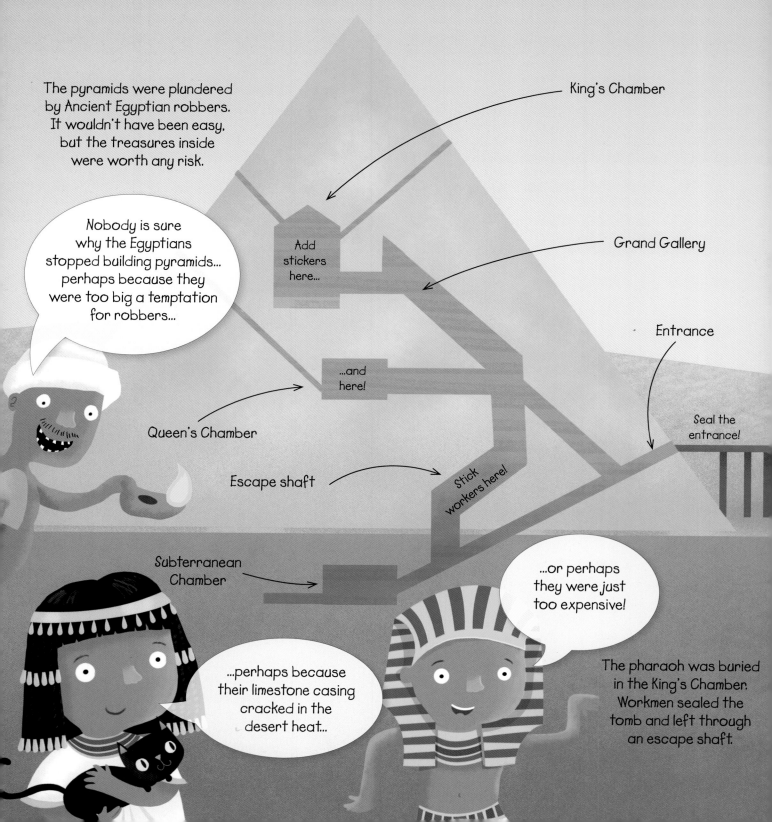

The pyramids were plundered by Ancient Egyptian robbers. It wouldn't have been easy, but the treasures inside were worth any risk.

King's Chamber

Nobody is sure why the Egyptians stopped building pyramids... perhaps because they were too big a temptation for robbers...

Add stickers here...

Grand Gallery

Entrance

...and here!

Queen's Chamber

Seal the entrance!

Escape shaft

Stick workers here!

Subterranean Chamber

...or perhaps they were just too expensive!

...perhaps because their limestone casing cracked in the desert heat...

The pharaoh was buried in the King's Chamber. Workmen sealed the tomb and left through an escape shaft.

The Great Sphinx

The Sphinx has the body of a lion and the head of a man. Carved from solid rock and enlarged with blocks of limestone, it was the largest statue in the ancient world, measuring over 236 feet long and 66 feet high. It still stands today, although its nose and beard were lost long ago.

Akhenaten—an unpopular pharaoh

Akhenaten was an unusual pharaoh. He changed his name from Amenhotep and built a new capital city called Akhetaten, with a huge statue of Aten—the god he wanted everyone to worship—instead of all the others! This wasn't very popular and his city and religious ideas were abandoned soon after his death.

Pharaohs (even female ones) wore false beards to make them look like the beardy god Osiris.

Akhenaten also had ideas about art... he thought it should look more realistic and lifelike.

Akhenaten's chief wife was the beautiful Nefertiti. Pharaohs had many wives, and their chief wife was often their sister!

Create your own Procession sticker scene!

Akhetaten city
1 mile

Crowning glory

Egyptian pharaohs wore crowns to show they were in charge. When Egypt became a single kingdom, around 3150 BC, the Double Crown (Pschent) combined the Red Crown (Deshret) of Lower Egypt and the White Crown (Hedjet) of Upper Egypt. The Blue Crown (Khepresh) is often called the "war crown," as pharaohs pictured in battle wore this one.

The vizier was the pharaoh's right-hand man, and the second most important person in the kingdom.

I'm wearing a headcloth called a "nemes." It wasn't a crown, but it symbolized royal power.

White Crown (Hedjet)

Stick the war crown here!

Red Crown (Deshret)

No crown has ever been found in a tomb. It seems that they were passed from pharaoh to pharaoh rather than buried.

Stick the Pschent crown here!

Crowns were decorated with a cobra, vulture, or both. These symbols were supposed to spit fire on the pharaoh's enemies!

Dressing to impress

This wealthy lady is getting ready for a royal banquet. Precious metals and stones were only for the rich, but many people could afford colorful "faience" jewelry. Jewelry was often decorated with charms called amulets that protected the wearer—for example fish amulets protected against drowning.

Perfumed cones of wax may have been worn for special occasions. They would have slowly melted, releasing their scent.

Pierced ears, wigs, and makeup were fashionable for both men and women.

The ugly god Bes protected the home. Egyptians thought that pulling faces, dancing, and being noisy protected against evil. Try telling your parents that!

Add a bronze mirror here!

Dress this lady in fine jewelry!

Bes

Stick a makeup pot here!

Stick a lotion jar here!

Colorful faience jewelry was made from crushing and heating crystals and minerals.

The tomb of Tutankhamun

Instead of building pyramids, later pharaohs hid their tombs in the hills of the remote "Valley of the Kings." Work started on a tomb as soon as a pharaoh came to power. Tutankhamun died young, in 1323 BC, so he was buried in a small tomb that was originally meant for someone else.

Tombs were never meant to be found. Entrances were blocked and hidden away. Some tombs had traps or hidden chambers to foil robbers!

Scenes of the afterlife and religious texts covered tomb walls. This tomb was finished in a hurry. Others were much grander!

Stick a completed panel here!

Walls were polished with stones, then plastered before decorating.

Stick a lamp here!

Stick a worker here!

Workers lived nearby, in the village of Deir-el-Medina. It was far from the Nile, so all food and water had to be brought in by donkeys.

Some of the 60 tombs in the *Valley of the Kings* are huge. The longest extends over 425 feet into the rock... that's a lot of digging!

Wooden adze

Stick a worker here!

Scarab beetles were symbols of regeneration and a popular design for amulets.

Gruesome mummification

Ancient Egyptians believed the spirit could only survive in the afterlife if the body was preserved. That's why they went to such extraordinary lengths to preserve the bodies of the pharaohs. It could take up to 70 days to get a pharaoh ready for burial!

Tutankhamun's inner coffin was pure gold. It took eight men to lift it!

How to make a mummy

1. Remove and dry internal organs. Leave heart for the gods to weigh.

2. Hook brain out through the nose and throw away. The brain's not thought to be useful for much...apart from making snot.

3. Dry body for up to 40 days in a mineral called "natron."

4. When dry, stuff body with sand or material to give it a more human shape. Onions were sometimes used as false eyes!

5. Wrap in layers and layers of oil-soaked linen. Add some magical amulets in the linen.

6. Wrap the bandaged mummy in linen sheets and tie with bandages.

7. Place a mask over the mummy's head. Congratulations, your mummy is now complete!

Stick the mummy's mask here!

Add hands holding crook and flail here!

Place the baboon lid here.

Place the jackal lid here.

Place the human lid here.

Place the falcon lid here.

Lungs

Stomach

Liver

Intestines

The spells on these canopic jars were thought to protect the body's organs.

The mummy was placed in its coffin by the Chief Embalmer. He wore the mask of Anubis, the god of mummification.

What to pack for the afterlife

Although Tutankhamun's tomb was broken into by robbers, it was resealed with most of its treasures and forgotten for thousands of years.

Annex

Food and wine were stored in the annex.

The treasury alone was filled with over 5,000 items...hurry up you lot!

Antechamber

Six chariots were placed in the tomb, they had to be taken apart to fit.

Overseer

Corrido

I hope someone left the instructions to put them back together again!

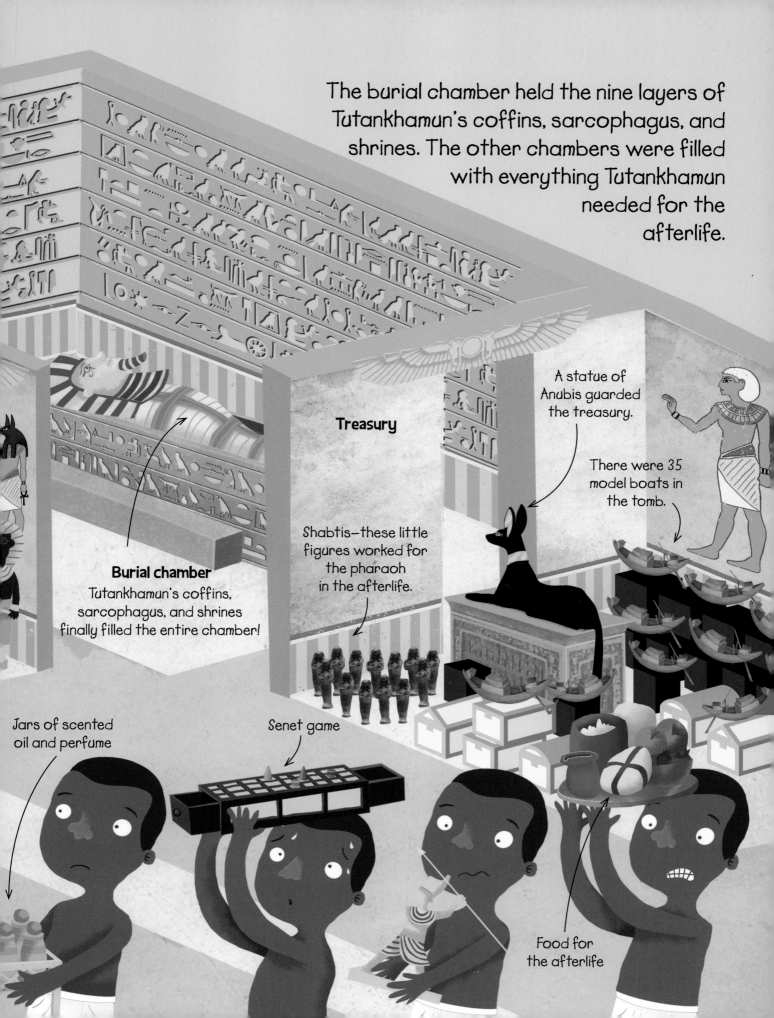

The burial chamber held the nine layers of Tutankhamun's coffins, sarcophagus, and shrines. The other chambers were filled with everything Tutankhamun needed for the afterlife.

Treasury

A statue of Anubis guarded the treasury.

There were 35 model boats in the tomb.

Shabtis—these little figures worked for the pharaoh in the afterlife.

Burial chamber
Tutankhamun's coffins, sarcophagus, and shrines finally filled the entire chamber!

Jars of scented oil and perfume

Senet game

Food for the afterlife

Create your own Tomb sticker scene!

Ramesses the Great and the Battle of Kadesh 1274 BC

Ramesses II is one of the most famous of all pharaohs. He fought many battles, including the Battle of Kadesh against the Hittites. The Egyptians were facing certain disaster, but Ramesses rallied his men and prevented a complete defeat. Back in Egypt, he made sure it was called a victory.

Ramesses built many huge temples and monuments, but he also added carvings to existing ones...to make it look as if he built them too.

Ramesses ruled for over 65 years. He boasted that he was father to 100 sons and 60 daughters!

Egyptian factories could make over 100 chariots per week!

Create your own Battle of Kadesh sticker scene!

The perilous journey to the afterlife

The journey to the afterlife wasn't easy! As well as passing gates guarded by terrifying supernatural monsters, the dead also had to swear that they had not committed a range of sins from, "I have not stolen," to the less-dreadful sounding, "I have not eavesdropped"! The final test was the "Weighing of the Heart."

The fertile Nile

Egyptian agriculture

Ancient gods

Everyday life

Djoser's giant steps

Great Pyramid sticker scene

The Great Sphinx

Inside the pyramid

Procession
sticker scene

Dressing to impress

The tomb of
Tutankhamun

Crowning
glory

Gruesome mummification

Tomb sticker scene

Battle of Kadesh sticker scene

The perilous journey to the afterlife